# FORM IN MODE

CW00382320

# FORM IN
# MODERN POETRY

by

## HERBERT READ

## VISION

VISION PRESS LIMITED
c/o Harper & Row Distributors Ltd.
Estover
Plymouth PL6 7PZ
ISBN 0 85478 336 9

British Library Cataloguing in Publication Data

Read, Herbert, *1893 – 1968*
Form in modern poetry
1. Poetry in English, 1900 – 1945 – – Critical studies
I. Title.
821'.912'09
ISBN 0-85478-336-9

© 1932 by Herbert Read
First published by Vision Press Ltd. 1948
Fourth impression 1964
Paperback edition 1989

*All rights reserved*

Printed in Great Britain by
Billing & Sons Ltd., Worcester
MCMLXXXIX

This essay was first published in the year 1932—at a time, that is to say, when we could look back with a sense of achievement on twenty years of vital poetic experiment. The period opened with the *Personae* and *Exultations* of Ezra Pound (1909); it continued with the *Responsibilities* of W. B. Yeats (1914), which announced the "conversion" of the greatest poet of the day; and its delineation was complete when T. S. Eliot published *Prufrock* in 1917. Thereafter it became a question of infiltration and consolidation, of explanation and patient elaboration. I need not detail the stages; I only wish to point out that this "apology" for modern poetry was written in a mood of quiet confidence which now, sixteen years later, might seem to have been premature.

There has been no recession among the pioneers. Whatever may be thought of the recent work of Ezra Pound, it cannot be described as a return to academic traditions; and however traditional Mr. Eliot may have become in his beliefs, his technique remains the technique of free verse in "the original meaning" of that phrase.* Why a later generation should have refused to follow where we led is no doubt a phase of history which some devotee of the dialectical method will one day explain. Poetic experiment, in the 'thirties, may have been rated as a diversionary activity; and the age demanded, so we were told, faith in all simplicity. If the simplicity had been Wordsworthian, or even Tolstoyan, we might have confessed

* That is to say, free verse as defined by Mr. Eliot in his Introduction to *Selected Poems of Ezra Pound*, 1928.

5

the error of our ways. But, in the event, the simple was the banal, and the faith an inhibitory political creed. When the props collapsed, as was inevitable, the retreat was Thermidorian. Not that there is anything bloody-minded or vindictive about your younger poets —they are apt to be all too full of admiration and respect for their elders. Nor is it necessary to deny them achievements of considerable value. They excel in metrical virtuosity, and the best of them remain interesting because they are intelligent. But below the best is an epiphytic tangle from which no individual growth emerges. One can only conclude that these poets have never stood where we stand, nor seen what we see, nor felt as we feel. I do not write in any vainglorious spirit; we are all implicated in what is best described as a " failure of nerve." The only excuse for reprinting this essay is that it might conceivably serve as a restorative; as a recall to rigorous experiment, to personal integrity, to the conditions of all great art.

*January,* 1948.                                   H.R.

## I

If a literary critic happens to be also a poet (*un poète manqué* is the usual taunt) he is liable to suffer from dilemmas which do not trouble the philosophic calm of his more prosaic colleagues. He may elaborate his theory and practice of criticism with perfect objectivity, looking on literature as so much material to be measured, compared and evaluated. That is the method of scientific criticism, and unless we confuse criticism with emotional impressionism, it must remain the ideal of all criticism. But the critic who is also a poet is in a special difficulty. With a certain objectivity he has elaborated his system of scientific criticism ; but at other moments in his life, in another mood, he has felt a creative urge, and submitting to this urge has written poetry which owes nothing to his critical theories. These poems, whether good or bad, are nevertheless events in his life, much more vivid than any rational notions he may have acquired from reading other people's poetry. When such a critic-poet attempts to probe down into such a fundamental question as the form and structure of poetry, he cannot escape the evidence of his own experience, but must in some way establish an agreement between his theory and his practice.

Save for such experiences in my own case, this essay might have been simpler than it is. I should have been able to adopt a definite attitude or join a traditional school. In a broad sense my theory of poetic form would have been either classical or romantic. Most definitely it would have been classical, but when I stand up squarely to the traditional terms

7

of classical theory, and attempt to relate them to my experience, I find there is no application—my experience cuts across the classical-romantic categorisation.

I find, in fact, that it is necessary to distinguish between two kinds of form, which I will call *organic* and *abstract*. The abstract is evolved from the organic; but it represents a fixation of the organic in a particular mode. Let me illustrate the point by an analogy drawn from the more objective plastic arts. When the nomadic hordes known as the Scythians invaded South Russia in the eighth century B.C., they brought with them an art, limited in range, consisting of various metal ornaments used in the decoration of harness, weapons and apparel. Such ornaments usually took the shape of very vigorous and lively representations of animals—stags, reindeer, lions, tigers and eagles. The designs were generally stylised; that is to say, the natural form of the animal was distorted in the interests of linear rhythm and dynamic effect. The form of such objects I should describe as organic; every departure from truth-to-nature is at the same time an intensification of natural vitality.

The Scythians settled in South Russia and their art developed in a normal way. We find that the animal motives which they had first used singly began, after an interval of two or three centuries, to be used in sterotyped combinations. They were confronted in pairs to form a antithetic design; they were arranged in rows and series, and in the most complicated type evolved by this simple people the animals are interlinked in a chain or spiral which makes a rhythmical pattern over the whole of the decorated surface—a symphony, as it has been called.

In the early Scythian animal style, the form is single, integral and organic. In the later style, the form is abstracted from the original impulse and made to serve as a unit in an arrangement which is not related to the original impulse, but is an abstract (numerical) arrangement of given units.

Let me now give a general definition of these two types of form :

*Organic form* : When a work of art has its own inherent laws, originating with its very invention and fusing in one vital unity both structure and content, then the resulting form may be described as *organic*.

*Abstract form* : When an organic form is stabilised and repeated as a pattern, and the intention of the artist is no longer related to the inherent dynamism of an inventive act, but seeks to adapt content to predetermined structure, then the resulting form may be described as *abstract**

It is then natural to ask whether these opposed entities of style correspond to any accepted categories in criticism. They may, I think, be directly related to the concepts ' romantic ' and ' classical,' provided these concepts are accepted in their proper, that is

* This corresponds roughly to the distinction which Coleridge, following Schelling, made between " organic form " and " mechanical regularity," but we can now see more clearly that it arises out of an evolutionary or historical development of art, and is not merely formalistic.

to say, their *historical,* sense. I wish to avoid these confusing terms as much as possible, though I think no confusion is necessary if we bear in mind the two distinct meanings of each term. In one case we can distinguish the meanings verbally, for ' classical ' may be reserved for the historical sense, whilst 'classicistic' serves for the derivative and sentimental sense; and perhaps we ought to be bold enough to use ' romanticistic' as well as ' romantic.' The terms in general have been given quite final definition by Sir Herbert Grierson in his Leslie Stephen lecture on " Classical and Romantic" (reprinted in *The Background of English Literature,* 1925), and I am . conscious of his definitions in the use I make of the terms in this essay.

The correspondence of organic and abstract forms with romantic and classical periods in the history of the plastic arts is obvious enough. The transition from the organic type to the abstract always coincides with the transition from a period of stress and energy to a period of satiety and solidity; and that is the historical distinction between romantic and classical periods. And it is quite clear that the classical and romantic periods are related to each other in a ' life-cycle ' which is the recurring cycle of the growth, maturity and decay of culture. But it is most important to remember that the term ' romantic ' especially is often restricted to an art based on sentiment, which may be typical of inferior classical as well as of inferior romantic periods. To be quite

10

clear, when referring to this type of romanticism, we might always call it ' sentimental-romanticism.'

The form which I propose to investigate in the following essay corresponds to the *organic unit* of the animal style in Scythian art, and more generally to the form typical of the romantic phase in any cultural development. It is the form imposed on poetry by the laws of its own origination, without consideration for the given forms of traditional poetry. It is the most original and most vital principle of poetic creation; and the distinction of modern poetry is to have recovered this principle. But before we can see how organic form takes shape, we must first consider the nature of the poet's personality; for upon the nature of his personality depends the form of his poetry.

## II

Many writers, especially novelists, have written in accordance with some theory of the nature of personality—George Meredith is an example—and an enquiry into such working theories would be of great interest. But that is an aspect of the subject which I should like to exclude from the present enquiry, which is to be concerned not so much with personality, as objectively conceived by the writer, as with the writer's own personality—the subjective nature of personality, the part it plays in the process of writing : what, briefly, we might call the creative function of the personality. This is, perhaps, a vague subject, but its very vagueness is the excuse I offer for dealing with it. If we can introduce a few definitions into this twilight, a good service to criticism will have been rendered. As it is at present, this word ' personality ' is tossed about, a more or less meaningless counter, from critic to critic. There is scarcely a literary judgment made anywhere in recent times that does not resolve itself into a statement such as : " The work of so and so is good because it is the perfect expression of his personality." This is not an exaggeration. I take the first book that comes to my hand. It is Volume I of the Cambridge Shakespeare, with a general Introduction by Sir Arthur Quiller-Couch. There I find this passage—three birds for a single stone :

" . . . who can doubt that every true man, small or great, leaves some print of himself on his work, or indeed that he *must* if his work be literature, which is so personal a thing. As Sir Walter Raleigh puts it, 'No man can walk abroad save on his own shadow.' Yes, but as another writer, Mr. Morton Luce, well comments, 'an author may be—perhaps ought to be—something inferior to his work'."

That reminds me of another passage, from *The Sacred Wood* of Mr. T. S. Eliot :

"Poetry is not a turning loose of emotion, but an escape from emotion; it is not the expression of personality, but an escape from personality."

"But, of course," adds Mr. Eliot, "only those who have personality and emotions know what it means to want to escape from these things"; and earlier in the same essay he has explained his meaning in these words :

"The point of view which I am struggling to attack is perhaps related to the metaphysical theory of the substantial unity of the soul : for my meaning is, that the poet has, not a 'personality' to express, but a particular medium, which is only a medium and not a personality, in which impressions and experiences combine in peculiar and unexpected ways. Impressions and experiences which are important for the man may take no place in the poetry, and those which become important in the poetry may play quite a negligible part in the man, the personality."

I do not quote these passages as texts, to attack or commend, but merely as illustrations of the use of the word 'personality' in modern criticism, and of the evident concern which critics have for its significance or otherwise. It will, however, be realised that the point of view of Mr. Eliot is a very exceptional one, and in fact a protest against a universal reliance on a vague concept. Mr. Eliot might hold that the notion of personality is *inevitably* vague; at least he does not attempt to define it. I think, however, that the attempt will be worth while.

We cannot hope to arrive at a definition of personality without encroaching to some extent on the science of psychology. Some of my readers will be uneasy at the prospect. Nevertheless, this is where I take my stand, even against my best friends in criticism, such as Mr. Eliot himself. I believe that criticism must concern itself, not only with the work of art in itself, but also with the process of writing, and the writer's state of mind when inspired —that is to say, criticism must concern itself, not only with the finished work of art, but also with the workman, his mental activity and his tools. If that is not admitted, no really useful progress can be made in this essay. But assuming we are agreed on the sphere of criticism, then I cannot conceive how the critic can avoid a dependence on general psychology. It may be said that psychology is a very doubtful science, and that none of its conclusions is established; but that is to set up as a better psychologist than the psychologists themselves. If we depart a single pace from the consideration of the work of art in isolation from all personal questions we involve ourselves in psychological considerations.

14

It might be possible, for example, to plunge into the quarrel of Romantics and Classics with nothing in our armoury but an objective measuring-rod. An infallible distinction might be found in the use of the letter ' p,' in feminine rhymes and false quantities; it would be infallible, but it would be dull. We should separate the sheep and goats, but the really interesting question—why some people are goats, and others sheep—that question would be left unsolved.

That is why, as a critic, I am tempted to seek an alliance with psychology, but I should like to distinguish between a general *entente*, and a treaty of obligations. As a literary critic—that is to say, as a scientist in my own field—I insist on maintaining my territorial rights when I enter into treaty with another science. I accept just as much as seems relevant to my purpose, and I reject anything that conflicts with the evidence of my own special sensibility. But actually, if the literary critic will approach psychology without prejudice, he will find certain important conclusions which are generally accepted by psychologists themselves, and which he can apply with great profit to his understanding of literature.

I will take as an example, because it is relevant to the enquiry I am making, the theory of the mind as developed by the psycho-analysts, particularly by Freud. I am aware that there are certain fundamental aspects of psycho-analysis which are hotly disputed by psychologists in general—particularly that part of the theory which supposes the existence

15

of an unconscious mind, or unconscious region of the mind. Now it happens that this particular hypothesis is the one which the literary critic is likely to be most tempted to adopt. Let him use every caution, for as one psychologist has warned us : " All usages of the term ' unconscious ' that imply that it is an entity, such as saying that ideas are *in the unconscious,* or that the unconscious is dynamic, show a thoughtless or uncritical attitude—or ignorance."* Freud himself, as we shall see, is not guiltless in this respect. I think, however, before we begin to criticise Freud, or even to use any of his terms, we should make sure that we know the meaning of them. It so happens, that in one of his essays,† Freud himself has given a concise résumé of his theory. He writes :

" The division of mental life into what is conscious and what is unconscious is the fundamental premise on which psycho-analysis is based; and this division alone makes it possible for it to understand pathological mental processes, which are as common as they are important, and to co-ordinate them scientifically. Stated once more in a different way : psycho-analysis cannot accept the view that consciousness is the essence of mental life, but is obliged to regard consciousness as one property of mental life, which may co-exist along with its other properties or may be absent."

* Henry Herbert Goddard, " The Unconscious in Psychoanalysis," *Problems of Personality* (1925), p. 300.
† *The Ego and the Id.* (Eng. tr. 1927).

Then Freud shows how we are compelled to adopt the concept of the ' unconscious ' :

" We have found—that is, we have been obliged to assume—that very powerful mental processes or ideas exist which can produce in the mind all the effects that ordinary ideas do . . . without themselves becoming conscious . . . this is the point at which psycho-analytic theory steps in with the assertion that such ideas cannot become conscious because a certain force is opposed to them, that otherwise they could become conscious, and that then one would see how little they differ from other elements, which are admittedly mental. The fact that in the technique of psycho-analysis a means has been found by which the opposing force can be removed and the ideas in question made conscious renders this theory irrefutable. The state in which the ideas existed before being made conscious is called by us *repression*, and we assert that the force which instituted the repression and maintains it is perceived as *resistance* during the work of analysis . . . We see, however, that we have two kinds of unconscious—that which is latent but capable of becoming conscious, and that which is repressed and not capable of becoming conscious in the ordinary way . . . That which is latent, and only unconscious in the descriptive and not in the dynamic sense, we call *preconscious;* the term unconscious we reserve for the dynamically unconscious-repressed . . . "

That is a long quotation, but it is essential to use these terms—'conscious,' 'preconscious' and 'unconscious'—and to use them in an accepted sense. The words as used by Freud have been subjected to criticism and he has not been afraid to revise his terms and make them more precise.

Freud says, in the work from which I have been quoting, that " in every individual there is a coherent organisation of mental processes, which we call his *ego* "; and this may serve as the *preliminary* definition of ' personality ' of which I am in search. This ego is identical with the conscious flow of our thoughts, the impressions we receive, the sensations we experience. Also, from this ego, this *coherent organisation* of mental processes, according to Freud, proceed the repressions " by means of which an attempt is made to cut off certain trends in the mind not merely from consciousness, but also from their other forms of manifestation and activity." Freud, following another Austrian writer, Georg Groddeck, further claims that the conduct of the ego throughout life is essentially passive—we are ' lived,' as it were, by unknown and uncontrollable forces. But presumably these forces are inherent, differentiated in each individual—being, in fact, that reserve of instincts and passions which normally we repress, but which are never securely under the control of our conscious reason. To this reserve Freud gives the name ' Id,' for it is the impersonal aspect of the ' Ego.'

Near to the word ' personality ' we have another

word, often used interchangeably with it, sometimes contrasted with it—I mean the word 'character.' This concept, too, we can bring into relation with the general scheme of Freudian psychology. Character can be explained as a disposition in the individual due to the repression of certain impulses which would otherwise be present in the personality; it is therefore something more restricted than personality. Character, which always has such a positive aspect, is really the result of certain fixities or negations imposed on the flow of consciousness. A flood only gains character and direction when it is confined between banks.

Before trying to show how the mind of the poet is related to these several concepts, let me draw confirmation of the rightness of Freud's general analysis of the mind from an unexpected quarter, a work first published at the beginning of our century and neglected until revived by Dame Ethel Smyth in 1930. *The Prison,* by H. B. Brewster, is a philosophic dialogue of great force and originality, and there I find this definition of the personality :

" We live in a web of associated memories; our general map—the chart thanks to which we know more or less clearly where to put what, recognize analogies, form classes, make order out of chaos and accumulate experience—is a network of memories. And one of ourselves, the loudest voiced one, the one we usually think of when we say *I,* corresponds to the spot on that map where the most frequent and familiar memories cross each other, as the railroads of a country at its capital."

It will be perceived how nearly this definition approaches Freud's conception of the ego as "a coherent organization of mental processes." Much more in Brewster's dialogue might be related to Freud's psychology; for example, that state of mind which Brewster opposes to the personality is nothing but Freud's unconscious 'id.'

It would be easy to give many further illustrations from literature which would give support to our preliminary definition of personality, but as they are so often bound up with, and even confused with, the notion of 'character,' we must first make a clear distinction between the two. The word 'character' derives from the Greek word meaning an engraved sign, a distinguishing mark; and in common usage it always implies a man moulded to a pattern, firm, consistent, dependable. Again, the use of the word for that literary form known as 'the character' and practised by Theophrastus, Vauvenargues and others, gives the same meaning; a consistent type. Descriptive psychologists adopt this same conception; the definition of Münsterberg may be quoted as typical. Character, he says, "is the power to keep the selected motive dominant throughout life." The difficulty about such a definition is that some 'power'—force, will or energy—is implied, for which there is no adequate theory of causation. The psycho-analysts have supplied this, and again I think their hypothesis is the most suggestive one for our purposes. They

regard inhibition as the basis of character, and a
definition which we may accept as representative is
that of Dr. Roback, which reads : " [Character is the
result of] an enduring psycho-physical disposition to
inhibit instinctive impulses in accordance with a
regulative principle."* Now there are various words
in that very condensed definition which need
explanation. Inhibition I have already referred to,
but if we do not care to accept it in its psycho-
analytical sense, I think it will do for our definition
if we merely regard the "disposition to inhibit" as
the " will to hold in check," in the ordinary moralistic
sense. Again, the phrase "instinctive impulses"
need not be given any but its normal meaning—
there are many instincts besides the sex instinct, and
if any one instinct is more in question than another,
I think it is probably the gregarious instinct. There
is a passage in that classical analysis of the character,
Meredith's *The Egoist,* which describes this aspect of
the problem very well :

" Within the shadow of his presence," Meredith
writes of Sir Willoughby Patterne, " he compressed
opinion as a strong frost binds the springs of earth,
but beyond it his shivering sensitiveness ran about
in dread of a stripping in a wintry atmosphere.
This was the ground of his hatred of the world ;
it was an appalling fear on behalf of his naked
eidolon, the tender infant Self swaddled in his name
before the world, for which he felt as the most

* "Character and Inhibition." *Problems of Personality,*
p. 118.

highly civilized of men alone can feel, and which it was impossible for him to stretch out hands to protect. There the poor little lovable creature ran for any mouth to blow on; and frost-nipped and bruised, it cried to him, and he was of no avail! Must we not detest a world that so treats us? We loathe it the more, by our measure of our contempt for them, when we have made the people within the shadow-circle of our person slavish."

This does not mean that the man who avoids the herd will thereby form his character; you do not inhibit an instinct by avoiding its activity. But the man who maintains a certain integrity in the midst of the herd, that man is by way of forming his character. Dr. Roback quotes very appositely Goethe's couplet :

> " *Es bildet ein Talent sich in der Stille* :
> *Sich ein Charakter in dem Strom der Welt.*"

" A talent is formed in solitude; a character in the stream of the world "*—a sentiment which I would ask the reader to remember because I am presently going to suggest that this difference between the conditions necessary for the formation of a character and for the formation of what Goethe calls a talent and what I am here calling a personality, corresponds precisely with the difference between rhetorical and lyrical literature, which is the difference often loosely

* Stendhal has said the same thing : *"On peut tout acquérir dans la solitude, hormis du caractère."* De l'Amour, Fragments Divers, I.

implied in the terms 'classical' and 'romantic' literature.

But first I must draw attention to the final clause in Dr. Roback's definition of character: it is "an enduring disposition to inhibit instinctive impulses *in accordance with a regulative principle.*" That, of course, implies that there is an element of self-determination in character. It is obvious that characters vary enormously in value, and I think a little consideration will show that the differences in value are due to differences in intelligence. A man without any intelligence, a lunatic, is a man most decidedly without any character. A man with a perverse intelligence, like Don Quixote, is a deformed character, a caricature of the real thing. Another negative aspect to remember is, that character once formed is not affected by experience. It is possible for groups of men to endure, over lengthy periods, the same experiences (I am thinking particularly of the experiences of war) and to emerge at the end of it with their characters not in the least changed. Character is in fact armour against experience; it is not in itself deflected by experience. From whatever direction we approach it, we get the notion of fixity; and once a man's character is determined, it is hardly possible to speak of his moral or spiritual development. A character is 'set,' 'hard-boiled' as the slang phrase vividly expresses it. Not even the emotions will dissolve it, or move it. The emotions indeed are irrelevant to character; they are waves which break themselves in vain against its base. History is full of examples of men of character who have exercised their justness and firmness in spite of the emotional claims of friendship and love.

Character, in short, is an impersonal ideal which the individual selects and to which he sacrifices all other claims, especially those of the sentiments or emotions. It follows that character must be placed in opposition to personality, which is the general-common-denominator of our sentiments and emotions. That is, indeed, the opposition I wish to emphasise; and when I have said further that all poetry, in which I include all lyrical impulses whatsoever, is the product of the personality, and therefore inhibited in a character, I have stated the main theme of my essay.

One problem absorbs me above all others: it is what I will call *the intermittency of genius*. Why, more often than not, does a poet blossom out in his adolescence and early manhood, and then wither to pedantry and dullness? Why does inspiration work fitfully and often at intervals of many years? Why, to put these questions in concrete terms, did Milton cease writing poetry for twenty-five years? Why did a poet like Gray write only one poem of supreme excellence? Why, for a brief decade, did the great poetic genius of Wordsworth pour out its richness, and then lapse into comparative poverty? One could ask a hundred questions of this kind, but the reader is not to imagine that I am going to provide a universal key to answer them all. I think, however, that this problem of the relations of personality to character does provide the right setting for such questions, and if psychology can solve *its* problem, then with the aid of psychology we shall be on the way to solving our own literary problem.

It would be too simple a solution to say that, character and personality being so opposed, inspiration will flow so long as the personality does not harden into character. In psychology you have always to reckon with the phenomenon of compensation. If you suppress one instinct, you revive another; we are infinitely complex machines, so that a check on one action is apt to release the spring of another action. The man of character may have repressed the conscious functioning of certain instincts; he cannot, however, prevent them from forcing their way underground into the preconscious and unconscious states described by Freud. The physical potentiality of the instincts remains in the body, though their surface workings may be suppressed. What is suppressed in consciousness may be found reactive in the imagination, which might be identified with the preconscious of Freud's phraseology. Dr. Jung confirms this supposition, remarking that "the unconscious feeling of the intellectual is peculiarly phantastic, often in grotesque contrast to an exaggerated, rationalistic intellectualism of the conscious. In contrast to the purposefulness and controlled character of conscious thinking, the feeling is impulsive, uncontrolled, moody, irrational, primitive, archaic indeed, like the feeling of a savage."*

* "Psychological Types." *Problems of Personality*, p. 300.

C            25

Along these lines I think, we might explain the art of certain intellectual types of the present day—I mean, in literature, the writings of the ' Surréalistes ' in France, of Franz Kafka in Germany, and even the later writings of James Joyce; and in painting, the art of men like Paul Klee and Max Ernst. Let me interpose here this axiom of criticism : by explaining the nature of a work of art, we do not explain it away. Art always rises superior to its origins. It is an entity of direct appeal; we do not, in the process of appreciation (no process but an immediate insight) unfold the process of creation.*

To return to my main argument : this phantasy proceeding from the unconscious as a balance or compensation for instincts repressed in the interests of character, may be identified with *fancy;* and this I think fits in well, not only with the modern types of art and literature already mentioned, but generally with the distinction between fancy and imagination in the literature of the past. For the sake of a tidy correspondence, it ought to be possible to relate *imagination* to the preconscious, and this I think can be done without much difficulty. But I must avoid, if only for lack of space, the endless controversy which revolves round these two words; I have, besides, on another occasion pointed out the relationship which exists between the intellect and fancy.†

* I have dealt more generally with the psycho-analytical approach to literature in an essay published in *Reason and Romanticism* (1926), pp. 83-106.
† *English Prose Style,* Chap. IX.

But now we must enlarge our description of *personality*. As a preliminary I have suggested that the term might be identified with Freud's ' Ego '—a coherent organisation of mental processes. But the coherence of this organisation is not to be confused with the fixed organisation of a character—any more than the coherence of a work of art is to be confused with the concision of a machine. The nature of this coherence is very well defined in an essay on personality by Mr. Ramon Fernandez.* He has been discussing Nietzsche's conception of personality, which he finds wanting in just this element of coherence.

" To be coherent," he explains, " does not mean that one *feels oneself* the same, nor *that one acts* in the same way in all circumstances, but rather that one is ready to meet every circumstance when once a certain inward perspective has been established; it does not mean that one never changes, but that the changes of the world always find you ready to select your own point of view . . . the more complicated the personality grows, the more unstable it becomes, and the more it submits to the influence of the mind . . . The ideal personality would be that of a man who showed himself ever capable of adapting his being to the movements of his thought, and whose thought would be ever in accord with the universal; who, in such conditions, considering himself with stern impartiality, would accept gladly

* *De la personnalité* (1928), pp. 86-87.

that idea which for the moment may take the lead; because thought which ceaselessly renews itself will make him—in Emerson's phrase, 'live always in a new dawn,' but at the same time it will prevent him from falling into incoherence, being guaranteed by its own laws."

Such a conception of personality is admittedly based on the most exact, the most complete and fearless revelation of a personality that we possess : Montaigne's Essays. I perhaps need quote* only one of a hundred passages in which this notion is put forth. It is a sufficiently famous one :

"What I do I do thoroughly, as a matter of habit, and make one step of it; and I seldom take any step that steals away and hides from my reason, and that is not very nearly guided by all my faculties in agreement, without division or inner revolt. My judgment takes all the blame or all the praise for it; and the blame it once takes it takes always, for almost from birth it has been one : the same inclination, the same direction, the same strength. And in the matter of general opinions, I have since my childhood occupied the position I had to hold."

It will be seen that in both authors we have the idea of a free disposition which is that of the sensations and memory—the sensual being—and that this being is given coherence, is defined or outlined, by a

* From the translation by E. J. Trechmann (Oxford, 1927), p. 266.

judgment which is innate. The ego is a synthesis of
the sensations, is generated by conscious experience,
by that inward perspective which Montaigne exercised so freely for our delectation. The judgment is
not imposed on the sensations from without, as if by
an external agency—that is the process of repression
which results in character; judgment emerges from
the history of our sensations, is elected by them, and
the coherence of personality is indeed the coherence
of a natural process; not the coherence of an arbitrary
discipline.

Mr. Fernandez's book, from which I have just
quoted, has much more to offer us that is suggestive;
its only fault, in my opinion, is that it tends to confuse
the coherence of the personality with the fixity of the
character; at least, it does not clearly mark off the
functions of character. But speaking of the restricted,
the too limited notion of personality in Corneille, he
gives us a perfect description of character—he
describes it as " the tragic conformity of a man to his
definition "—Freud would say " to his ' ego-ideal.' "
The personality knows no such definitions, no such
ideal; it is an active process of thought, a balance
of relations maintained between our various feelings
and sentiments. From this process, this play of
thought, comes a certain act of belief, the *illative*
act described by Newman. The nature of belief
in general is not a subject to embark on now.*

* It has been the subject of a very adequate enquiry by
the Reverend M. C. D'Arcy, S.J.—*The Nature of Belief*
(London, 1931).

I would merely suggest that the reality of the personality—its operative efficiency—is dependent on a belief in the existence of the self, a belief that may have little support in objective evidence, but is made possible by that ontological faith, that belief in the continuity of experience, which is the will to live. This is, you will see, a state of mind very different from that involved in character : the whole difference between blind compulsion to an external and arbitrary ideal, and an organic coherence intuitively based on the actual world of sensation.

I should like for my last illustration to pass from Mr. Fernandez to a friend of his whose work he has criticised so intelligently : I mean Marcel Proust. Proust's great work rivals Montaigne's in the deliberate light it throws on this problem of personality.

" Frequent discussions with Marcel Proust," writes Mr. Fernandez (p. 23), " who would adopt instantaneously no matter what point of view, have revealed to me that man dehumanizes himself by excess of affectivity at least as much as by excess of rationality . . . To wish to introduce unity into the life of sensation and affectivity, by separating out one's sentiments and giving them a structure without ever leaving the level of concrete life, was not that precisely to put oneself in quest of a personality ? "

Proust was very much occupied by this problem of personality and gave most attention to the very aspect of the problem that I now wish to consider here—I

mean the extent to which the personality depends on
the memory, and particularly on the memory of
sensations. There is a famous excursus, coming
almost exactly in the middle of Proust's long epic,
which is a key to the author's whole philosophy of art
and life. He has just related how, in a moment of
complete physical collapse, there comes to him, by
an instinctive act of recollection, the living image of
his grandmother; and it is only at this moment,
more than a year after her burial, that he becomes
conscious that she is dead. This causes Proust to
reflect that " at whatever moment we estimate it,
the total value of our spiritual nature is more or less
fictitious, notwithstanding the long inventory of its
treasures, for now one, now another of these is un-
realisable, whether we are considering actual treasures
or those of the imagination "—or those actually of the
memory. Then Proust goes on to make this very
significant, and for his work, quite essential analysis
of the personality :

" For with the cloudiness of memory are closely
linked the heart's intermissions. It is, no doubt,
the existence of our body, which we may compare
to a jar containing our spiritual nature, that leads
us to suppose that all our inward wealth, our past
joys, all our sorrows, are perpetually in our posses-
sion. Perhaps it is equally inexact to suppose that
they escape or return. In any case, if they remain
within us, it is, for most of the time, in an unknown
region where they are of no service to us, and

where even the most ordinary are crowded out
by memories of a different kind, which preclude
any simultaneous occurrence of them in our consciousness.  But if the setting of sensations in
which they are preserved be recaptured, they
acquire in turn the same power of expelling every
thing that is incompatible with them, of installing
alone in us the self that originally lived them.*

Mr. Fernandez is very critical of this passage and
therefore of Proust's method in general.  He does not
deny its acuteness, nor its significance—for Proust.
But far from being the key to Proust's genius, he
regards it as a confession of Proust's weakness.  Mr.
Fernandez's criticism at this point would be much
clearer if it were combined with a distinction between
personality and character; as it is, the inadequacy of
Proust's analysis is impugned against such notions as
the integrity of our sentiments, our ideals, our spiritual
progress.

"If Proust is to be believed," Mr. Fernandez
writes, "not only can man not guarantee his
sentiments, and consequently his acts, and consequently man must be an eternal failure, but also
he must renounce the consolation of feeling that
he progresses despite this discontinuity and this
intermittent blindness . . .  It is the problem of
spirituality, of the value of the ideal, of the future
and of human progress, that is set by the Proustian
analysis of the intermissions of the heart . . . If

* *Cities of the Plain* by Marcel Proust, translated by C. K.
Scott Moncrieff.  Vol. I, p. 219.

the intermissions of the heart and their corollaries
represent the depths of human nature, the supreme
experience of our ego, then the spiritual life must
be ranged in its entirety in the category of the
imagination, and the intelligence is the highest point
of human development to which we may pretend
. . . the victory of the intelligence would mark the
defeat of the spirit."

But is so much implied in Proust's analysis? It is,
I think, true that, as Proust says elsewhere, the
respect for moral obligations, faithfulness to friends,
the achievement of a task, the observance of a discipline, have a surer foundation in blind habits than
in the momentary and ardent flights of our sensibility. But is this not equivalent to saying that
character as we have defined it is formed by the
inhibition of the instinctive life—that, put inversely,
the full and free life of the personality must be sacrificed in the interests of any fixed ideals, whether of
morality or the imagination? But does this mean
that no alternative progress is possible for the personality? That is the momentous question to which we
are finally driven, and which I will now try to answer.
It may have been noticed how closely Proust's
analysis agrees with Freud's. It is the phenomena of
the mind in its conscious, unconscious and even preconscious phases of repression and censorship, that
Proust is describing in words not far removed from
the scientific vocabulary of psycho-analysis. But I
doubt very much that Proust had any exact know-

ledge of psycho-analysis; at many points we must regard his work as a confirmation, or an anticipation, of the observations of Freud. Proust speaks of the heart, and Freud of the mind; but these are interchangeable concepts.

I will not carry the parallel any farther. But I do wish to point out how closely Proust's description of the intermissions of the heart can apply to that other parallel phenomenon—the intermissions of genius, or inspiration, to which I have already referred. We all have our moments of inspiration, and perhaps they differ, as between an ordinary mortal and a genius, only in the degree of their intensity. Poets have not often described their creative experiences, but there is one account, quoted by Mr. Percy Lubbock in his Introduction to the *Letters of Henry James,* that is quite unique in the beauty and fulness of its revelation. Henry James began one night to feel his way towards a novel which he had in mind, and among the working notes for this novel were found some pencilled lines from which I should like to quote the essential passage :

" Infinitely interesting—and yet somehow with a beautiful poignancy in it that makes it strange and rather exquisitely formidable, as with an unspeakable deep agitation, the whole artistic question that comes up for me in the train of this idea . . . of the donnée for a situation that I began here the other day to fumble out. I mean I come back, I come back yet again and again, to my only seeing it in the dramatic way—as I can only see everything and anything now; the way that filled my mind and floated and uplifted me when a fortnight ago I gave my few indications to X. Momentary side-winds—things of no real authority—break in every now and then to put their inferior little questions to me; but I came back, I come back, as I say, I all throbbingly and yearningly and passionately, oh mon bon, come back to this way that is clearly the only one in which I can do anything now, and that will open out to me more and more, and that has overwhelming reasons pleading all beautifully in its breast. What really happens is that the closer I get to the problem of the application of it in any particular case the more I get *into* that application, so that the more doubts and torments fall away from me, the more I know where I am, the more everything spreads and shines and draws me on and I'm justified of my logic and my passion . . . Causons, causons, mon bon—oh, celestial, soothing, sanctifying process, with all the high sane forces of the sacred time fighting through it, on my side! Let me fumble it gently and patiently out—with fever and fidget laid to rest—as in the old enchanted months! It only looms, it only shines and shimmers, *too* beautiful and too interesting; it only hangs there too rich and too full and with too much to give and to pay; it only presents itself too admirably and too vividly, too straight and square and vivid, as a little organic and effective Action . . ."

Referring to this confession, Mr. Lubbock says : "It is as though for once, at an hour of midnight silence and solitude, he opened the innermost chamber of his mind and stood face to face with his genius." I think, in the consistent phraseology I have tried to adopt, we might say that in such a mood of creative activity, the author stands face to face with his personality. He stands fully conscious of the wavering confines of his conscious mind, an expanding and contracting, a fluctuating horizon where the light of awareness meets the darkness of oblivion ; and in keeping aware of that area of light and at the same time watching the horizon for a suggestion of more light, the poet induces that new light into his consciousness ; as when, at twilight, no stars are visible to a casual glance, but shine out in answer to a concentrated stare. Such lights come, of course, from the latent memory of verbal images in what Freud calls the preconscious state of the mind ; or from the still obscurer state of the unconscious, in which are hidden, not only the neural traces of repressed sensations, but also those inherited patterns which determine our instincts. But it is not inspiration alone—not the sudden ingress of light—which makes the poet ; that is only the intermission which, if isolated, leads to an easy despair. The essential faculty is an awareness of one's own personality, and the capacity to cultivate its inherent activities " without division or inner revolt," as accurately described by Montaigne. Montaigne was not a poet, though he might have been an inspired novelist. But that is beside the point ; what distinguishes one kind of artist from another is not their states of mind, their mental machinery, but a difference in the distribution of sensational development—the difference, that is to say, between a poet and painter is a difference between verbal-aural and plastic-visual sensibility; a difference of material, not of method. And that, it seems, is another way of saying with Mr. Eliot that "the poet has, not a 'personality' to express, but a particular medium, which is only a medium ... in which impressions and experiences combine in peculiar and unexpected ways."

It looks, therefore, as though the one thing an artist must avoid is the fixity of character. This conclusion is forced on us from still another point of view. A man of character is generally distinguishable as a man of action. Or as Keats wrote in a letter to his friend Bailey (22nd Nov., 1817):

"Men of Genius are great as certain ethereal Chemicals operating on the Mass of neutral intellect—but they have not any individuality, any determined Character—I would call the top and head of those who have a proper self Men of Power."*

If we say that there is a fundamental opposition between the artist and the man of action, the statement is acceptable enough. At least, it would fit typical artists like (to mention only poets) Shakespeare and Blake. It would explain the sudden

* *Letters* (Oxford, 1930), p. 72.

withering of Wordsworth's genius : he acquired a character. But what of Milton and Goethe? Well, of Milton we can say that he was a poet of one kind in his youth, that he then became a man of action and was silent for twenty-five years, and then became a poet once more, but of a different kind. Of Goethe I cannot speak with any confidence, but I suspect that a complete analysis might reveal a real poet and a real personality, but a somewhat fictitious character. Finally—to repeat a suggestion I have already made—may we not perhaps explain the dreary quarrel of romantic and classic as an opposition between two kinds of art, springing respectively from personality and from character? It is an explanation that would work out very well in practice. We have only to think of Dryden and of Dr. Johnson, and to compare them with Shakespeare and Keats.

The only objection which I can foresee to this theory of personality in literature is the one raised in a general way by Mr. Fernandez : it does not account for the moral and intellectual development in a poet like Shakespeare. Between *Romeo and Juliet* and *Measure for Measure*, between *Hamlet* and *The Tempest*, there is a vast difference which we can only call, in Nietzsche's phrase, a transvaluation of all values. But the poet and his poetry remain the same. The medium, the material—all pedantry apart —is one. But then must we conclude, because a man of character is an admirable spectacle, in his fixity of demeanour and directness of action, a type to be envied and imitated, that therefore this other type of man, this mobile personality of which poets are made, can show no compensating virtues? Must we not rather conclude that the virtues of personality inhere in its very mobility? * For though thought by its own nature is capable of development, it can be implemented by the whole personality, and therefore made real, only when that personality is free to adapt itself to the movements of thought. Thought and personality go hand in hand, and their goal, whether confessed or not, is that state of vision or revelation which all great spirits have attained.

* Its " negative capability " as Keats called it in a letter to his brothers (28th Dec., 1817) :
" I had not a dispute, but a disquisition, with Dilke upon various subjects; several things dove-tailed in my mind, and at once it struck me what quality went to form a man of achievement, especially in literature, and which Shakespeare possessed so enormously—I mean *Negative Capability,* that is, when a man is capable of being in uncertainties, mysteries, doubts, without any irritable reaching after fact and reason. Coleridge, for instance, would let go by a fine isolated verisimilitude caught from the Penetralium of mystery, from being incapable of remaining content with half-knowledge."—*Letters* (Oxford, 1930), p. 77.

## III

In one of his lectures on Shakespeare, Coleridge defined the principle of modern poetry in these words :

" No work of true genius dares want its appropriate form, neither indeed is there any danger of this.  As it must not, so genius can not, be lawless : for it is even this that constitutes its genius—*the power of acting creatively under laws of its own origination.*"

By ' modern ' poetry I mean all genuine poetry from Coleridge's day to ours—and indeed all genuine poetry of all time.   But because people have no clear definition of poetry, and because a very different kind of activity has too often usurped the title of poetry, this principle has been obscured.  It thus comes about that every poet who strives for this principle—from Wordsworth to Hopkins or Mr. Eliot—has to wear the trappings of a rebel, and what is the assertion of a law of discipline is treated as a declaration of independence.

No further progress can be made in this essay without a direct statement on the nature of poetry. This cannot have the exact proportions of a logical definition.    Poetry is properly speaking a transcendental quality—a sudden transformation which words assume under a particular influence—and we can no more define this quality than we can define a state of grace.  We can only make a number of distinctions, of which the main is the broad but elemental one between poetry and prose.   I use the word elemental deliberately, because I believe the difference between poetry and prose to be, not one of surface qualities, not of form in any sense, not even of mode of expression, but absolutely of essence. It is not a case of the mind, in need of expression, choosing between two ways—one poetry, the other prose. There is no choice for the particular state of mind in which poetry originates. It must either seek poetic expression, or it must simply not be expressed; for an altogether lower tension, involving a different kind of mentality, must be substituted before the activity of prose expression can intervene.

I do not wish to imply by these words any particular theory of æsthetics. The difference in tension really corresponds to a difference in the historical evolution of language. Poetry is a more primitive mode of expression than prose, and that is why the language of primitive peoples often seems poetic to us. And we have now, thanks to the labours of Lévy-Bruhl, abandoned the idea that what is primitive is necessarily inferior. In the circumstances in which they operate, the mind and language of the savage are more effective than the mind and language of the civilised man. But the world of one is not the world of the other, nor is the world of poetry the world of prose. The point of view I am expressing has probably been worked out in most detail and force by Vico (*Scienza Nuova*, Book II, Chaps. II and III); the following summary by his disciple Croce makes this clear :

" Poetry is produced not by the mere caprice of pleasure, but by natural necessity. It is so far from being superfluous and capable of elimination, that without it thought cannot arise: it is the primary activity of the human mind. Man, before he has arrived at the stage of forming universals, forms imaginary ideas. Before he reflects with a clear mind, he apprehends with faculties confused and disturbed : before he can articulate, he sings : before speaking in prose, he speaks in verse : before using technical terms, he uses metaphors, and the metaphorical use of words is as natural to him as that which we call ' natural.' "*

I have, in the preceding section of this essay, put forward a theory of the poet's personality which has some justification in modern psychology and is supported by the experience of various imaginative writers. The theory of poetic form which follows has been worked out on the basis of my own practice, and on the basis of my own vivid experience of the presence of poetic values in other poets. I want to keep the discussion as far as possible to a practical level. But I have found considerable support for my theories not only in Vico, but in more recent philosophy. There is some support in Croce, for the theory I advance necessarily assumes an intuitive quality in all art; but there is more in the works of another Italian, Leone Vivante, whose two books,

* *The Philosophy of Giambattista Vico.* By Benedetto Croce. Trans. by R. G. Collingwood (London, 1913), p. 48.

*Intelligence in Expression* and *Notes on* **the** *Originality of Thought,* are unduly neglected; but perhaps both Croce and Vivante owe a good deal to Vico and De Sanctis. The relevance of some of Signor Vivante's observations may be judged from the following paragraphs :

" In the poetic period not only the attribute, but every word, every moment of thought, gathers up, renews the whole. The subject is recalled in its concept in every word of the proposition, that is, it progressively takes fresh value, fills up of itself and governs every new moment. Thus reality at every point is drawn up from the unknown. The new expressive moment in its particular significance forms itself in the meaning of the whole, which in the new moment is not inferred but renewed : and myriads of *nexus*—resemblances, accords, unities, *ex principio*—form themselves. On the other hand, constructive thought loses the *nexus* or necessities of principle proper to thought in its integral originality : if we except the *nexus* belonging to formal logic, to a conception schematically material and spatial—a position of mere existences and of spatial and quantitative relations and ideal abstract identities. In other words, in constructive thought *nexus of inherence* are comparatively prevalent, in poetic thought *nexus of essence.*"*

* *Notes on the Originality of Thought* (The Bodley Head, 1927) pp. 164-5.

"In prose the period is more subject to rules, whether in the collocation of words, in the structure of the phrase, or in the use of words; *i.e.*, it is subject to conventional usage. Uncommon words can hardly be introduced; it seems wayward and arbitrary to use them, and in general we cannot depart from common usage—while in poetry a like transgression,' a like inversion or the uncommon use of a word passes, as such, unobserved. And this is due to the boldness which words have in poetry—because their meaning is entirely present, their every reason or value is present and active in them, in every moment of expression; and because, on the other hand, the very material, as it were, calls forth activity to form itself according to all its intrinsic values and forms and, being one with activity, is itself concept."[*]

All art originates in an act of intuition, or vision. But such *intuition* or vision must be identified with *knowledge*, being fully present only when consciously objectified. This act of vision or intuition is, physically, a state of concentration or tension in the mind. The *process* of poetry consists firstly in maintaining this vision in its integrity, and secondly in expressing this vision in words. Words are generally (that is to say, in prose) the *analysis* of a mental state. But in the process of poetic composition words rise into the conscious mind as isolated objective 'things' with a definite equivalence in the poet's state

[*] *Intelligence in Expression* (C. W. Daniel, 1925), p. 3.

of mental intensity. They are arranged or composed in a sequence or rhythm which is sustained until the mental state of tension in the poet is exhausted or released by this objective equivalence.

To this description of the process of poetry there is one qualification to make. If we take it at its bare worth, it might be held to justify those theories of 'pure poetry' which have had much vogue lately. These theories imply that the intuition or vision of the poet is expressed simply by a *musical* equivalence in the words. This I think may be possible in isolated words and phrases, particularly those of a high-sounding 'proper' meaning ("In Xanadu did Kubla Khan . . ."), but poetry in general disproves the theory of pure poetry. Words, their sound and even their very appearance, are, of course, everything to the poet : the sense of words is the sense of poetry, but words have associations carrying the mind beyond sound to visual image and abstract idea. And the poet, even as he becomes conscious of words in the act of composition, feels them tincturing his consciousness not only with sound, but also with colour and light and power—in short, with meaning. Poetry depends, not only on the sound of words, but even more on their mental reverberations.

So much by way of a theoretical preamble. Historically, I believe that this theory of poetry is illustrated by the main tradition of English poetry which begins with Chaucer and reaches its final culmination in Shakespeare. It is contradicted by most French poetry before Baudelaire, by the so-called

classical phase of English poetry culminating in
Alexander Pope, and by the late Poet Laureate. It
was re-established in England by Wordsworth and
Coleridge, developed in some degree by Browning
and Gerard Manley Hopkins, and in our own day by
poets like Wilfred Owen, Ezra Pound and T. S. Eliot.

The distinction is not merely that between
' classical ' and ' romantic.' This division cuts across
in a different direction. The real distinction is
between the poetic process as I have defined it, and a
process adequately described by Dryden as *wit-
writing.* In the Introductory Letter to *Annus
Mirabilis* Dryden wrote :

> " The Composition of all poems is or ought to
> be of wit; and wit in the Poet, or *Wit writing,*
> (if you will give me leave to use a School dis-
> tinction), is no other than the faculty of imagination
> in the Writer; which, like a nimble Spaniel, beats
> over and ranges through the field of Memory, till
> it springs the Quarry it hunted after; or, without
> metaphor, which searches over all the Memory for
> the Species or Ideas of those things which it designs
> to represent. *Wit written* is that which is well
> defin'd, the happy result of Thought, or product
> of Imagination."

And further :

> " The first happiness of the Poet's Imagination
> is properly Invention, or finding of the thought;
> the second is Fancy, or the variation, deriving or

moulding of that thought as the Judgment represents it proper to the subject; the third is Elocution,
or the Art of clothing and adorning that thought so
found and varied, in apt, significant and sounding
words. The quickness of the Imagination is seen
in the Invention, the fertility in the Fancy, and the
accuracy in the Expression."

This is an excellent description of the practice of
Dryden and of others of his school, and that the
practice results in a verbal art of a high order, no
one would deny. But such art is not poetry; it is no
more than elocution, or, as we should now say,
eloquence.

To give but one illustration :

" Will all great Neptune's ocean wash this stain
Clean from my hand; no, this my hand will rather
The multitudinous seas incarnadine
Making the green one red."

—Which is poetry. But the following lines are wit-
writing, or eloquence :

" Lo ! thy dread empire, Chaos ! is restor'd;
Light dies before thy uncreating word;
Thy hand, great Anarch ! lets the curtain fall,
And universal darkness buries all."

I think Wordsworth was the first poet to be fully
conscious of the difference between poetry and wit-
writing, and his various Prefaces contain admirable
definitions of the nature of poetry. These definitions

are of great psychological exactitude, but since they are consistent with the general theory of poetry already enounced (and indeed, the main inspiration of it), and since I have dealt with them in detail in a book on Wordsworth,* I will not review them now. It is sufficient to emphasise the historical fact, that Wordsworth emancipated himself and the whole tradition of English poetry from the prevailing tyranny of wit-writing, which had lasted for about a century and a half.

Wordsworth's restorations (one cannot speak of innovations, for there is nothing new in Wordsworth that is not to be found in the Ballads, or in Shakespeare and Milton), were confined to the sphere of what he called poetic diction. He saw, and saw rightly, that the defect of wit-writing was fundamental, and therefore to be sought in the very act of composition. He concuded that it was a *verbal* defect—and this verbal defect he identified with artificiality. All his efforts were concentrated on this end : the return to naturalism and simplicity of diction. But he was only partially right. Artificiality was only one of the symptoms of the disease. The real defect involved the state of the poet's mind in its completeness, and was reflected, not only in diction, but also throughout the whole poetic process —in modes of feeling, in diction, rhythm and metre. Wordsworth's mode of feeling was fully involved : to be exact, we should say that it was a divergence in

* *Wordsworth* (1931). A new edition (Faber and Faber) in the press (1948).

his emotional reactions to experience (arising out of his experiences in France in 1792) that was the primary cause of his dissatisfaction with the poetry of the eighteenth century (to which he had hitherto been devoted). To his changed emotional outlook, the wit-writing of Dryden and Pope would naturally appear as so much "gaudiness and inane phraseology." But if he had looked deeper, he would have found that more than phraseology was involved. It will now be seen that what precisely was involved was the whole theory of personality and character which I have been outlining in this essay.

Nevertheless, the course of poetry in the nineteenth century was determined by Wordsworth. Not one poet—not Shelley nor Keats, not Landor nor Tennyson, not even Swinburne—but was affected by the revolution in poetic diction originated by Wordsworth. They were affected, but did little to develop the situation as Wordsworth left it. Against the magnitude of Wordsworth's experiment, all the minor tinkerings of the nineteenth century are as nothing—until we come to Browning and Gerard Manley Hopkins. Browning had no particular theory of diction : he wanted his verse to be expressive, and expressive it was—of his personality. But what he did do was considerably to enlarge the scope of poetry by adding certain categories of content to it, such as those embodied in his dramatic monologues and his psychological studies generally. His influence is important because its tendency is to encourage an objective attitude in the poet. Matthew

Arnold should perhaps not be passed over; he adds little to Wordsworth's achievement, but he did experiment in free verse, and the originality that is claimed for contemporary writers of free verse is excessive unless *The Strayed Reveller* is borne in mind. But that graceful experiment bore little fruit. Hopkins's experiments, however, were of far greater potential influence, and must be considered in more detail.

Gerard Manley Hopkins was born in 1844, and died in 1889. He may therefore be reckoned as a contemporary of Swinburne, by whom he was perhaps momentarily influenced. But while Swinburne has had his fiery ascension, and now scarcely smoulders, Hopkins has only just emerged from the darkness to which his original genius condemned him. It is a familiar story; nothing could have made Hopkins's poetry popular in his day : it was necessary that it should first be absorbed by the sensibility of a new generation of poets, and by them masticated to a suitable pulp for less sympathetic minds. That process is going on apace now, and when the history of the last decade of English poetry* comes to be written by a dispassionate critic, no influence will rank in importance with that of Gerard Manley Hopkins.

Hopkins himself was aware of the quality of his genius, and therefore knew what to expect from his contemporaries. Even in his undergraduate days at Oxford, he could write :

* I was referring, at the time of writing, to the decade 1921-30.

" It is a happy thing that there is no royal road to poetry. The world should know by this time that one cannot reach Parnassus except by flying thither. Let from time to time more men go up and either perish in its gullies fluttering excelsior flags or else come down again with full folios and blank countenances. Yet the old fallacy keeps its ground. Every age has its false alarms."

The most obvious false alarm, as I have already suggested, was Swinburne; but he was of the number who perish in the gullies of Parnassus. More false, because more seeming-fair, are those who come down again with full folios and blank countenances, and among these can be numbered some of Hopkins's closest friends. Probably the only one of his small circle who understood him fully was his fellow-poet, Richard Watson Dixon. Dixon, writing to Hopkins to urge him to write more poems, refers to their quality as " something that I cannot describe, but know to myself by the inadequate word *terrible pathos*—something of what you call temper in poetry : a right temper which goes to the point of the terrible : the terrible crystal. Milton is the only one else who has anything like it, and he has it in a totally different way; he has it through indignation, through injured majesty, which is an inferior thing . . ." Here is a full understanding which we do not find in the published letters and writings of others who knew Hopkins—not in Coventry Patmore, who floundered in deep astonishment, and not in his closest friend

and final editor, the late Poet Laureate. To contend
that Dr. Bridges did not understand the poetry of
Hopkins would not be quite fair; he understood the
craftsmanship of it, and was sensible to the beauty.
But there seems to have been an essential lack of
sympathy—not of personal sympathy, but of sympathy in poetic ideals. The Preface to the notes which
Dr. Bridges contributed to the first edition of the
poems (reprinted in the new edition of 1930) is
marked by a pedantic velleity which would be
excusable only on the assumption that we are dealing
with a poet of minor interest. That is, indeed, the
attitude : " Please look at this odd fellow whom for
friendship's sake I have rescued from oblivion." The
emphasis on oddity and obscurity is quite extra-
ordinary, and in the end all we are expected to have
is a certain technical interest, leading to tolerance,
and the discovery of " rare masterly beauties."
Hopkins is convicted of affectation in metaphor,
perversion of human feeling, exaggerated Marianism,
the " naked encounter of sensualism and asceticism
which hurts the *Golden Echo*," purely artistic wanton-
ness, definite faults of style, incredible childishness in
rhyming—at times disagreeable and vulgar and even
comic; and generally of deliberate and unnecessary
obscurity. Everything, in such an indictment, must
depend on the judge's set of laws, and in criticising
Dr. Bridges's treatment of Hopkins, I am wishing to
say no more than that the Poet Laureate applied a
code which was not that of the indicted. The lack of
sympathy is shown precisely in this fact. Hopkins was

a revolutionary; that is to say, his values were so fundamentally opposed to current practices that only by an effort of the imagination could they be comprehended. Once they are comprehended, many apparent faults are justified, and there is no reason to dwell on any of them.

Hopkins was serene and modest in his self-confidence. He could admit the criticism of his friends, and yet quietly persist in his perverseness. To one of them he wrote, in 1879 :

" No doubt my poetry errs on the side of oddness. I hope in time, to have a more balanced and Miltonic style. But as air, melody is what strikes me most of all in music and design in painting, so design, pattern, or what I call *inscape* is what I, above all, aim at in poetry. Now it is the virtue of design, pattern, or inscape to be distinctive, and it is the vice of distinctiveness to become queer. This vice I cannot have escaped."

And again, a little later :

" Moreover, the oddness may make them repulsive at first sight and yet Lang might have liked them on second reading. Indeed, when, on somebody returning me the *Eurydice,* I opened and read some lines, as one commonly reads whether prose or verse, with the eyes, so to say only, it struck me aghast with a kind of raw nakedness and unmitigated violence I was unprepared for : but take breath and read it with the ears, as I always wish to read, and my verse becomes all right."

A full exposition of Hopkins's theories would take us far into a discussion of the historical development of poetry. Let me briefly indicate their main features. There is in the first place a metrical theory, of the greatest importance. Hopkins's poems are written in a mixture of what he called Running Rhythm and Sprung Rhythm. Running rhythm, or common English rhythm, is measured in feet of either two or three syllables, and each foot has one principal stress or accent. Hopkins preferred to take the stress always first, for purposes of scanning; but obviously that is only a question of convenience. To vary this running rhythm, poets have introduced certain licences, of which the chief are reversed feet and reversed rhythm. If you pursue these variations far enough, the original measure will seem to disappear, and you will have the measure called by Hopkins sprung rhythm. In this measure each foot has one stress, which falls on the only syllable, if there is only one, or on the first if there are more than one. Normally there should not be more than four syllables to a foot, and the feet are regular, measured in time. Their seeming inequality is made up by pause and stressing.

In general, sprung rhythm, as Hopkins claimed, is the most natural of things. He tabulated the reasons :

(1) It is the rhythm of common speech and of written prose, when rhythm is perceived in them.

(2) It is the rhythm of all but the most monotonously regular music, so that in the words of

choruses and refrains and in song closely written
to music it arises.

(3) It is found in nursery rhymes, weather saws,
and so on; because, however these may have been
once . made in running rhythm, the terminations
having dropped off by the change of language, the
stresses come together and so the rhythm is sprung.

(4) It arises in common verse when reversed or
counterpointed, for the same reason.

These reasons need no further comment; but there
are two historical considerations to note.    Sprung
rhythm is not an innovation; it is the rhythm natural
to English verse before the Renaissance.    It is the
rhythm of *Piers Plowman* and of Skelton.    Greene
was the last writer to use it, and since the Elizabethan
age, as Hopkins claimed, there is not a single, even
short poem, in which sprung rhythm is employed as a
principle of scansion.    The other observation Hopkins
could not make, because it is part of our history since
his time.    It is that the principles contended for by
Hopkins on the basis of scholarship and original
tradition (but only *contended* for on that basis : he
actually wrote as he felt, and then went to history to
justify himself) are in many essentials identical with
the principles contended for by those modern poets
already mentioned (whose advocacy and practice of
' free verse ' is also based on feeling and intuition
rather than historical analysis).

A second characteristic of Hopkins's poetry which,
while not so original, is yet a cause of strangeness,

may be found in his vocabulary. No true poet hesitates to invest words when his sensibility finds no satisfaction in current phrases. Words like " shive-light ' and ' firedint ' are probably such inventions. But most of Hopkins's innovations are in the nature of new combinations of existing words, sometimes contracted similes, or metaphors, and in this respect his vocabulary has a surface similarity to that of James Joyce. Examples of such phrases are to be found in almost every poem : ' the beadbonny ash,' ' fallowbootfellow,' ' windlaced,' ' churlsgrace,' ' footfretted,' ' clammyish lashtender combs,' ' wild-worth,' and so on. Commoner phrases like ' beetle-browed ' or ' star-eyed ' are of the same kind, made in the same way, and freely used by him. Here again an explanation would take us far beyond the immediate subject; for it concerns the original nature of poetry itself—the emotional sound-complex uttered in primitive self-expression. Mr. Williams, whose more graceful and appreciative introduction to the second edition of the poems is a fair corrective to the pedantic undertones of Dr. Bridges, has an excellent description of the phenomenon as it appeared in the composition of Hopkins's verse :

" It is as if the imagination, seeking for expres-sion, had found both verb and substantive at one rush, had begun almost to say them at once, and had separated them only because the intellect had reduced the original unity into divided but related sounds."

Poetry can be renewed only by discovering the original sense of word formation : the words do not come pat in great poetry, but are torn out of the context of experience; they are not in the poet's mind, but in the nature of things he describes.

" You must know," said Hopkins himself, " that words like *charm* and *enchantment* will not do : the thought is of beauty as of something that can be physically kept and lost, and by physical things only, like keys; then the things must come from the *mundus muliebris;* and thirdly they must not be markedly old-fashioned. You will see that this limits the choice of words very much indeed."

Of Hopkins's imagery, there is not much in general to be said, but that ' not much ' is all. He had that acute and sharp sensuous awareness essential to all great poets. He was physically aware of textures, surfaces, colours, patterns of every kind; aware acutely of earth's diurnal course, or growth and decay, of animality in man and of vitality in all things. Everywhere there is passionate apprehension, passionate expression and equally that passion for form without which these other passions are spendthrift. But the form is inherent in the passion. For, as Emerson remarked with his occasional deep insight, " it is not metres, but a metre-making argument, that makes a poem—a thought so passionate and alive, that, like the spirit of a plant or an animal, it has an architecture of its own, and adorns nature with a new thing."

The thought in Hopkins's poetry tends to be over-laid by the surface beauty. But the thought is very real there, and as the idiom becomes more accepted, will emerge in its variety and strength. There is no explicit system, nor need there be in great poetry. Perhaps the only essential quality is a sense of values, and this Hopkins had in a fervid degree. He was a convert to Roman Catholicism, and might have ranged widely in intellectual curiosity had he not pre-ferred to submit to authority. One of his con-temporaries at St. Beuno's Theological College wrote of him :

" I have rarely known anyone who sacrificed so much in undertaking the yoke of religion. If I had known him outside, I should have said that his love of speculation and originality of thought would make it almost impossible for him to submit his intellect to authority."

Perhaps in actual intensity his poetry gained more than it lost by this step, but one cannot help regretting the curtailment it suffered in range and quantity. After joining the Church, he applied to himself a strict ascetic censorship, and apart from what he may have destroyed, deliberately refrained from writing under every wayward inspiration. His remarkable criticism of Keats, in a long letter to Coventry Patmore published by Father Lahey,*

* *Gerard Manley Hopkins.* By G. F. Lahey, S.J. (Oxford, 1930).

shows what a high standard of intellectual and moral rectitude he expected in a poet :

"It is impossible," he says of Keats, "not to feel with weariness how his verse is at every turn abandoning itself to an unmanly and ennervating luxury."

In another kind of critic such a judgment would be excessively priggish; but in Hopkins it was a principle he lived by. His poetry is nothing if not intellectually tempered, virile, masculine, ' the terrible crystal,' the very opposite of all that is sentimental and indulgent.

Any more complete history of the evolution of modern verse technique would have to find a place for other poets—for Whitman, who contributed nothing very intelligent to its technical development, but rather a blind emotional force; for W. B. Yeats, whose later poetry is anything but conventional in its diction; for T. E. Hulme and Ezra Pound. It was with the school which Hulme started and Pound established that the revolution begun by Wordsworth was finally completed. Diction, rhythm and metre were fully emancipated from formal artifice, and the poet was free to act creatively under laws of his own origination. It was not always understood that, having cast off the tyranny of obsolete laws, the poet was under the necessity of originating his own, and much of the free verse that has been practised since 1914 compromises the theory by its feebleness. Nevertheless, the theory is right, and all true poetry of to-day, as all true poetry of the past, conforms to it. For, properly understood, this theory is not the theory of a particular school; it is the theory of all essential English poetry.

## IV

It might be objected that whilst this theory of poetry may be accepted as a theory of poetic essence, it will not account for poetry in being, which involves, besides essence, embodiment and structure. The question is : how can the poet pass from the metaphor and the lyric poem which is in reality no more than an extended metaphor, to those larger epic conceptions by which we measure the greatness of poets? To discuss the length of poetry might seem at first sight a very trivial approach to a serious subject. But actually it involves those first principles of the poetic faculty which we have been discussing. Most poets aspire to write long poems, and we might almost say that the distinction between a major and a minor poet is the capacity to write a long poem successfully I cannot think of any poet whom one would venture to call 'major,' whose work consists entirely of short pieces; though naturally there are many minor poets, with an exquisite talent for short pieces, who have many long, dreary and unreadable poems to their discredit.

How long is a long poem? is the simple question that might first be asked. The *Divine Comedy* and *Paradise Lost* are poems of the first order, and they are extremely long. The characteristic poems of Chaucer, Shakespeare, Dryden, Pope, Wordsworth, Shelley and Robert Browning are of comparable length. But is *The Ancient Mariner* a long poem? And the *Ode : Intimations of Immortality* or *Lamia*? Is Donne's *Progress of the Soul*, or Mr. Eliot's *Waste Land*? Obviously there is no general rule, and in the absence of a linear measure, we are driven to seek a qualitative one. Between the short poem and the long poem there is a difference, but it is not so much a difference of length as of essence.

The difference really turns on the question of lyricism. We often call the short poem a *lyric,* which meant originally a poem short enough to be set to music and sung for a moment's pleasure. From the poet's point of view, we might define the lyric as a poem which embodies a single or simple emotional attitude, a poem which expresses directly an uninterrupted mood or inspiration. A long poem, it would follow as a corollary, is one which unites by artifice several or many such emotional moods; though here the artifice might imply a single dominating *idea* which in itself might be an emotional unity.

In this short paragraph we have used several terms which are far more significant than a casual reading would reveal. I want especially to stress the words *emotion* and *idea,* in their particular contexts. It might be found that they are the very words which, dominating the nature of a poem, lead to the essential distinction we wish to make between a long poem and a lyric. But before breaching that essential distinction, there are certain descriptive features to be disposed of. For example, of the long poems already mentioned, some are properly described as epics, others as philosophic, some are odes and some are direct narratives. *The Canterbury Tales* are long because they could not very well be shorter : the poet has a series of stories to tell in verse, and he uses his verse

with economy and despatch to achieve the end. Such
length in a poem is at once necessary and arbitrary;
it is a necessity of the content, but so far as the poetic
quality of the poem is concerned, the length is
arbitrary; I mean, it is not the poetry that makes for
the length, but the story.

Most epic poetry is of this nature, though ' epic '
is not an exact term. The *Iliad* is an epic in one
sense; *Paradise Lost* in quite another sense. The
*Iliad*, like the *Canterbury Tales,* is lengthy by reason
of its story; and so, I think, is all true epic poetry.
But Milton, in his poem, had more in mind than the
story; the story of the Fall is merely the kernel, or
theme, round which he elaborates, firstly, a dramatic
myth, and secondly, a philosophical thesis. Here
the epic, we might say, is dominated by an idea;
though in the construction of a dramatic myth
another faculty is involved, which I will discuss
presently.

I confess I have never understood what precisely
an ode is. It is difficult to find anything in common
between Cowley's *Ode : Of Wit* and Dryden's *Ode on
St. Cecilia's Day* and, say, Wordsworth's *Ode :
Intimations of Immortality.* An ode, in practice
implies a certain architectonic mastery of rhythmic
variations; a structure which, I suppose, has its
analogies in music, but which, from a strictly poetic
point of view, does not differ from the long poem in
general; just as, from the point of view of eating, a
wedding cake terraced like a tabernacle does not differ
from plain plum cake. The ode, that is to say, is not

essentially long or short; it might conceivably be a lyric, as I believe Wordsworth's *Ode* to be.

It will be said that the philosophic poem, such as *De Rerum Natura,* the *Divine Comedy,* and, to take a modern example, *The Testament of Beauty,* does not need to be discussed at this point because it is obviously not lyrical in nature, and is invariably long. But what are we to say of a poem like *The Phœnix and the Turtle,* not a long poem by any means, but decidedly a philosophical one : indeed, a poem in which all the force and beauty of this kind of poetry is distilled in purest essence? There are many poems of Donne's, too, which superficially are lyrical in form, but philosophical in content. If only negatively, the philosophic poem shows that the difference between the long poem and the short poem is not to be found in the nature of its content.

Let us consider a final possibility : that there is no poetic difference between the long poem and the short poem : that there is a certain art of poetry, which arises we do not quite know how, from the music of vowels and consonants, the sound and associations of words, the surprise of images and metaphors; in the now consecrated phrase, that there is 'pure poetry,' and that the rest is prose, or padding. According to this theory, most poems would tend to be short, if only for the sufficient reason that it is impossible for any poet to sustain his inspiration for long; and actually, when the advocate of 'pure' poetry is pressed for examples, he can only quote you a few short lyrics, perhaps *Kubla Khan,* and for the rest, nothing but disinterred lines and couplets. I have already pointed out the general limitations of this theory : it is actually a species of solipsism. It confuses the thing and its attributes. It ignores what the world has agreed to call poetry in favour of an *a priori* definition of poetry. For what the advocate of ' pure ' poetry is defining is not poetry, but only a species of poetry, namely, ' pure ' poetry. Let us admit, even, that word-music, image and metaphor are the blood-stream of poetry, without which it cannot for a moment exist. Yet beyond these are structure and conception—structure which is the embodiment of words in a pattern or form; and conception, which is the projection of the poet's thought into a process from which, or during the course of which, words are generated.

That is to say, there can be no words with their accompanying music, no images with their visual immediacy, no metaphors with their more-than-verbal meaning, unless there is either an intuition of form, which I take to be an emotion about fitness, size, appropriateness, tension, tautness and so on (as in the sonnet); or, not alternatively so much as in addition, a progressive invention which will carry the poet on from word to word, line to line, stanza to stanza, book to book, until the invention is exhausted.

Form and conception are present in the lyric, but they are unobtrusive; the duration of the poetry is so short, the emotion so immediate (and relatively simple) that we do not perceive (it is the poet's business to conceal) the time-structure. Form and conception are fused in the act of creation. When form dominates the conception (that is to say, when the conception is limited enough to be seen as a single unit—to be held from the beginning to the end in one mental tension), then the poem can be defined properly as ' short.' On the other hand, when the conception is so complex that the mind must take it in in disjointed series, finally ordering these series in a comprehensive unity, then the poem is properly defined as ' long.'

In a successful sonnet, for example, or in *Kubla Khan*, the music of the first words has not died in the mind when the last words sound; nor is the configuration of the poem—its rhythm and closed form—for a moment lost. Its total effect is not only in the sound, but also in the shape. But in the long poem, the music is an accompaniment which is never lost, which is not coextensive with the form. It is the difference between the still beauty of a lake, looked at as a whole; and the beauty of the stream which we follow from its source to the sea, never seeing it at one time as a whole, but always aware of its continuity, its sameness in variation, its music in progression.

Having made this distinction and leaving the short poem on one side, we can perhaps ask a very relevant question : is the long poem worth while? It is a banal question, but necessary, because the long poem is very often attempted. It would be too rash to assume that it was extensively read ; in fact, we know that in general the reading public is bored with the long poem. But is it the fault of the length of the poem, of the long poem in itself; or are the long poems given to us in some sense unsuccessful? And in any case, if no one reads them, why do poets go on writing them?

There is a passage in another of Keat's letters which answers this last question. Writing to his friend Bailey in 1817, he says:

" I have heard Hunt say and I may be asked : why endeavour after a long poem? To which I should answer : Do not the Lovers of Poetry like to have a little Region to wander in where they may pick and choose, and in which the images are so numerous that many are forgotten and found new in a second Reading—which may be food for a week's stroll in the summer? Do not they like this better than what they can read through before Mrs. Williams comes down stairs? a Morning work at most. Besides a long Poem is a test of Invention which I take to be the Polar Star of Poetry, as Fancy is the Sails, and Imagination the Rudder. Did our great Poets ever write short Pieces? I mean in the shape of Tales—This same invention seems indeed of late years to have been forgotten as a Poetical excellence."*

Invention, fancy, imagination—here are terms which we have already used in another context perhaps with another meaning. What I think Keats

* *Letters,* I, pp. 55-6.

means, if I may venture to transpose his ideas into words which seem more consistent with the present argument, is that the long poem is a test of inspiration —though inspiration, which may on occasion mean motivation, is far from being a satisfactory word. That is to say, Keats thought that if the inspiration of the poet could hold out without flagging until it has embodied many moods and feelings *throughout the course of a narrative,* then the reader, in his turn, would find in the poem, not merely a single and momentary impression of loveliness, but a vast assembly of verses and images through which he may wander and find, now one sympathetic response, now another, according to his mood or feeling. In one case (the lyric) the poet immediately subdues the reader, and achieves his desired effect; in the other (the long poem), he drops his jewels in a chosen path, and allows the reader to pick up any that may catch his eyes.

From the poet's point of view, the long poem means, according to the view expressed by Keats, charging the narrative with a certain density or opacity. This is achieved by a liberal use of epithets, similes and metaphors, which, though poetic in themselves, may have the effect of impeding the narrative. Take almost any passage from *Hyperion* :

" In pale and silver silence they remain'd,
   Till suddenly a splendour, like the morn,
   Pervaded all the beetling gloomy steeps,
   All the sad spaces of oblivion,

And every gulf, and every chasm old
And every height, and every sullen depth,
Voiceless, or hoarse with loud tormented streams
And all the everlasting cataracts,
And all the headlong torrents far and near,
Mantled before in darkness and huge shade,
Now saw the light and made it terrible.
It was Hyperion :—a granite peak
His bright feet touch'd, and there he staid to view
The misery his brilliance had betray'd
To the most hateful seeing of itself.
Golden his hair of short Numidian curl,
Regal his shape majestic, a vast shade
In midst of his own brightness, like the bulk
Of Memnon's image at the set of sun
To one who travels from the dusking East :
Sighs, too, as mournful as that Memnon's harp,
He utter'd, while his hands, contemplative,
He press'd together, and in silence stood."

As a static poem it is very beautiful; as a piece of narrative it is halting, and the interest, surfeited with conceits, is apt to lag for the action. If from the passage you omit lines 4-11, 19-20, you do not injure either the descriptive force or the narrative action.

It is perhaps hardly fair to compare Keats and Chaucer, for there is a clash between romantic and realistic values. But let us take a passage from Spenser's *Faerie Queene* :

" There in a gloomy hollow glen she found
A little cottage, built of stickes and reedes

In homely wize, and wald with sods around,
In which a witch did dwell, in loathly weedes,
And wilfull want, all carelesse of her needes;
So choosing solitarie to abide,
Far from all neighbours, that her deuilish deedes
And hellish arts from people she might hide,
And hurt far off vnknowne, whom euer she
   enuide.

The Damzell there arriuing entred in;
Where sitting on the flore the Hag she found,
Busie (as seem'd) about some wicked gin:
Who soone as she beheld that suddein stound,
Lightly vpstarted from the dustie ground,
And with fell looke and hollow deadly gaze
Stared on her awhile, as one astound,
Ne had one word to speake, for great amaze,
But shewd by outward signes, that dread her
   sence did daze.

At last turning her feare to foolish wrath,
She askt, what deuill had her thither brought,
And who she was, and what vnwonted path
Had guided her, vnwelcomed, vnsought?
To which the Damzell full of doubtfull thought,
Her mildly answer'd: Beldame be not wroth
With silly Virgin by aduenture brought
Vnto your dwelling, ignorant and loth,
That craue but rowme to rest, while tempest
   ouerblo'th.

With that adowne out of her Christall eyne

Few trickling teares she softly forth let fall,
That like two Orient pearles, did purely shyne
Vpon her snowy cheeke; and therewithall
She sighed soft, that none so bestiall,
Nor saluage hart, but ruth of her sad plight
Would make to melt, or pitteously appall;
And that vile Hag, all were her whole delight
In mischiefe, was much moued at so pitteous
     sight."

Here nothing can be omitted without detracting from the descriptive force of the whole passage. There is only one simile in the four stanzas—"like two Orient pearls"—and this is too short, too vivid and too just to do anything but enhance the movement of the narrative. This does not mean that the passage from Spenser is better *poetically* than the passage from Keats; it merely means that Spenser's is the better *narrative* poetry; but if the object of the poem is to narrate, I think we might say that it is a better poem.

My point is, that Keats was mistaken in his approach to the long poem, and that both *Endymion* and *Hyperion* are failures as narrative poems just because Keats was trying to do something which cannot legitimately be done. He was misusing a definite form of poetry. His poems may be compared with motor-cars moving slowly in procession at a Carnival of Flowers, which must be stripped of their lovely decorations before they can resume their proper speed.

It must not be imagined, however, that all the virtue of a narrative poem lies in its efficiency in forwarding the action. Prose is sufficient for the purpose. Poetry always, in every kind, resides in the word and its associations. In narrative poetry the words must convey the action with speed and economy, but they must be fine emotive words; words such as we find, indeed, in the passage I have quoted from Spenser.

A narrative poem, then, may properly be called a long poem, but only in virtue of the content. The story is told, is perhaps invented; the poetry springs into being as the story unfolds. The story is the inspiration (and in this case also the motivation) of the poetry. The length of the poem is not motivated by the force of the poetic inspiration; but the poet will be poetically inspired by the narrative to the extent that he visualises the event of the narrative, and is moved by the visualisation. He will be moved so long as, in the famous phrase, he keeps his eye on the objects, on the visualised events.

But that does not achieve Keats's purpose in writing a long poem, which is to have "a little Region to wander in." Invention, which he calls the Polar Star of Poetry—surely this is not merely the capacity to tell a story? Is it possible that there are other modes of poetry, which satisfy Keats's purpose, but which are neither lyrical nor narrative? What of that other kind of poem, whose characteristic it is to be dominated by an idea?—

" An Orphic song indeed,
A song divine of high and passionate truths
To their own music chaunted."

That was Coleridge's conception of the long poem,
the ideal he quoted to Wordsworth* to explain his
disappointment with the *Excursion*. He tells us what
he had expected :

> . . . the colours, music, imaginative life, and
> passion of *poetry;* but the matter and arrangement
> of *philosophy;* not doubting from the advantages
> of the subject that the totality of a system was not
> only capable of being harmonised with, but even
> calculated to aid, the unity (beginning, middle and
> end) of a poem. Thus, whatever the length of the
> work might be, still it was a *determinate* length; of
> the subjects announced, each would have its own
> appointed place, and excluding repetition, each
> would relieve and rise in interest above the other."

" The totality of a system "—the phrase somehow
does not call up poetic associations. The famous
poem of Lucretius is perhaps the only one that is at
once systematic in the sense desired by Coleridge,
and also poetic. Coleridge discusses Lucretius, and
in this very context he utters his famous judgment
that Lucretius was most poetic when he was least
philosophical, and most philosophic when he was least
poetical. I have been inclined to accept this dictum

* Letter of May 30, 1815.

of Coleridge's as expressing a very probable truth, but lately it has been claimed, by one whose capacity to appreciate Latin poetry is far greater than mine,* that Coleridge's dictum needs considerable qualification : in fact, it is based on the narrow lyrical notion of poetry which we are now examining.    For in major poetry, as Matthew Arnold was so eager to point out, expression occupies a subordinate rank.† He quotes Goethe's opinion, that what distinguishes the artist from the mere amateur is Architectonicé in the highest sense : that power of execution which creates, forms, and constitutes; not the profoundness of single thoughts, not the richness of imagery, not the abundance of illustration.  The modern poet, says Arnold, has three things to learn from the classical writers of the ancient world :

"He will learn from them how unspeakably superior is the effect of the one moral impression left by a great action treated as a whole, to the effect produced by the most striking single thought or by the happiest image.  As he penetrates into the spirit of the great classical works, as he becomes gradually aware of their intense significance, their noble simplicity, and their calm pathos, he will be convinced that it is this effect, unity and profoundness of moral impression, at which the ancient Poets aimed; that it is this which constitutes the grandeur of their works, and which makes them immortal."

* Hugh Sykes Davies in *The Criterion*, September, 1931.
† Preface to 1852 edition of his Poems.

Arnold, it will be remembered, applied this test to Keats; dismissing *Endymion* as " so utterly incoherent, as not strictly to merit the name of a poem at all," he fixed his attention on *Isabella, or the Pot of Basil.* Admitting that " this one short poem contains, perhaps, a greater number of happy single expressions which one could quote than all the extant tragedies of Sophocles," he yet asks :

" But the action, the story? The action in itself is an excellent one; but so feebly conceived by the Poet, so loosely constructed, that the effect produced by it, in or for itself, is absolutely null."

Arnold, I think, effectively discounts Coleridge. We may doubt whether the totality of a system, or any purely philosophic theme, can be made the subject of a poem (necessarily a long poem) unless it is translated into action or imagery. It is the quality of the emotion that is really involved. By far the easiest method of securing the necessary emotional tension throughout the length of a ' long ' poem is to embody its theme in a dramatic myth, which is the way of Milton in *Paradise Lost.* The only other method is to secure a consistent and continuous vitality of expression by the operation, in every line of the poem, of a dominant emotion. This is the way of Lucretius in *De Rerum Natura.* Poetry of any length is visual or it is tedious; it may be visual by virtue of its action, or by virtue of its imagery. It can never, whilst still remaining poetry, be merely informative or conceptual.

It is for this reason that I think it is dangerous to admit, as Lascelles Abercrombie does in *The Idea of Great Poetry*, that the far richer and greater effects of the long poem can be achieved " by means of a unity far less direct," and " a form less immediately impressive and, therefore, no doubt, less lovely " than the means employed in a successful sonnet. There are really no degrees of poetry; at least, there is no easy transition from poetry to prose. The two forms of expression are distinct in kind, we must speak in either one mode or the other. It is not enough even to be ' visual '; prose can be ' visual.' Poetry must be visual in a swift, intuitive way. It must also, by its daring, adventure into a world of sense and sound beyond the reach of the mundane instruments of prose. That is its faculty of Invention, about which Keats speaks. Invention and Imagery—Poetry is an essence distilled by these emotional activities. But it is not an essence which we can dilute with the water of prose, to make it go a long way. There are many varieties of poetic expression, just as there are many voices that sing; but none of them forgoes its proper harmony.

## V

If I am right in my analysis of the poet's personality and of the consequent nature of poetic form, it is obvious that our critical values, in relation to the poetry of the past, must be radically revised. That, however, is not a task which I propose to undertake; I have already made a first essay,* but not, I now recognise, with all the courage my convictions demand. But the past can wait. I am more concerned for our immediate poetic practice. If the modern poet could learn to value his 'negative capability,' then something in the nature of oppression would lift from his mind and our native poetic genius might enjoy a new life. But I do not wish to end on vague notes of hope and aspiration; it is not a question of creating in the void. It is much more a question of re-establishing contact with a lost tradition, the tradition of our poetry from Chaucer to Daniel; the tradition, too, of Shakespeare. But Shakespeare is there to show us that tradition is a meaningless abstraction for the poet himself—" an irritable reaching after fact and reason." Almost daily I lift my voice in thanksgiving for this immortal witness : a poet who was no pedant nor moralist, a man of no character nor convictions, of no caste nor culture, but just a naked sensibility living in its own gusto, reaching after nothing more distant than the impassioned accents of its own voice as it issued from the " terrible crystal " of an intuitive mind. Let me add still another quotation from Keats, who knew

* *Phases of English Poetry* (London, 1928).

77

so well the true nature of the poet, and died on the point of revealing this knowledge in his poetry :

" As to the poetical Character itself (I mean that sort of which, if I am anything, I am a Member; that sort distinguished from the Wordsworthian or egotistical sublime; which is a thing per se and stands alone) it is not itself—it has no self—it is every thing and nothing. It has no character—it enjoys light and shade; it lives in gusto, be it foul or fair, high or low, rich or poor, mean or elevated. It has as much delight in conceiving an Iago as an Imogen. What shocks the virtuous philosopher, delights the chameleon Poet. It does no harm from its relish of the dark side of things any more than from its taste for the bright one; because they both end in speculation. A poet is the most unpoetic of anything in existence; because he has no Identity—he is continually in for* and filling some other Body. The Sun, the Moon, the Sea and Men and Women who are creatures of impulse are poetical and have about them an unchangeable attribute—the poet has none; no identity—he is certainly the most unpoetical of all God's Creatures. If then he has no self, and if I am a Poet, where is the Wonder that I should say I would write no more? Might I not at that very instant have been cogitating on the Characters of Saturn and Ops? It is a

* *Sic;* "informing" for "in for" has been suggested as an emendation.

wretched thing to confess; but it is a very fact that not one word I ever utter can be taken for granted as an opinion growing out of my identical nature—how can it, when I have no nature? When I am in a room with People if I ever am free from speculating on creations of my own brain, then not myself goes home to myself : but the identity of every one in the room begins so to press upon me that I am in a very little time annihilated—not only among Men; it would be the same in a Nursery of children. . . ."*

Along with this confession I should like to quote a similar passage from the autobiographical journal of a modern German poet, Rainer Maria Rilke :†

"Verses are not, as people imagine, simply feelings; they are experiences. In order to write a single verse, one must see many cities, and men and things; one must get to know animals and the flight of birds, and the gestures that the little flowers make when they open out to the morning. One must be able to return in thought to roads in unknown regions, to unexpected encounters, and to partings that had been long foreseen; to days of childhood that are still indistinct, and to parents whom one had to hurt when they sought to give one some pleasure which one did not understand (it would have been a pleasure to someone else);

* *Letters,* I, p. 245.
† *The Notebooks of Malte Laurids Brigge.* By Rainer Maria Rilke. Trans. by John Linton. (Hogarth Press, 1930.)

to childhood's illnesses that so strangely begin
with such a number of profound and grave trans-
formations, to days spent in rooms withdrawn and
quiet, and to mornings by the sea, to the sea itself,
to oceans, to nights of travel that rushed along
loftily and flew with all the stars—and still it is
not enough to be able to think of all this.   There
must be memories of many nights of love, each
one unlike the others, of the screams of women in
labour, and of women in childbed, light and
blanched and sleeping, shutting themselves in.
But one must also have been beside the dying,
must have sat beside the dead in a room with
open windows and with fitful noises.   And still it
is not enough to have memories.   One must be
able to forget them when they are many, and one
must have the immense patience to wait until they
come again.   For it is the memories themselves
that matter.   Only when they have turned to
blood within us, to glance and gesture, nameless
and no longer to be distinguished from ourselves—
only then can it happen that in a most rare hour
the first word of a poem arises in their midst and
goes forth from them."

These two descriptions of the poetic process are
complementary.   Keats stresses the receptive nature
of the poet's personality—its waywardness, its lack
of fixity, its lack of solidity.   Rilke shows how the
experiences of such a receptive nature become a com-
post of his blood and being, and only then emerge
fused in the poetic *word*.

We return, therefore, to our original distinction between character and personality, and the relevance of this distinction to poetic sensibility and poetic activity. I have tried to define the essential nature of poetry. I have shown how its very existence depends on the ' negative capability ' of the personality, and how incompatible it is with the ' positive capability ' of the character. If I left my theory at this stage, it would, I confess, leave an impression of inadequacy. There is, one must admit, some truth in Arnold's charge of incoherence against *Endymion*. Keats was a romantic poet; so, for that matter, was Rilke. Is all the evidence I have brought forward in favour of a theory of poetry and of the poetic personality anything but a concession to the romantic theory of poetry?

I took care, it will be remembered, in the section dealing with the psychology of character and personality, to suggest a principle of coherence in the personality, and I should like in conclusion to return to this principle in the light of our subsequent discussion of the nature of poetry. Mr. Fernandez, in the passage which I quoted on page 27, and which is very significant for my whole argument, relates the coherence of the personality to the coherence of thought—thought which is guaranteed by its own laws, thought which is ever in accord with the universal. The whole structure, not merely of this particular theory of poetry, but of the philosophy of life upon which it is based, would fall to pieces unless related to a belief in what Santayana has called a realm of essence; the highest poetry is inconceivable without the intuition of pure Being as well as the sense of existence. The poet must, if my contentions are right, live in the fleeting moments of vision, but in these moments his vision penetrates very deep and far, and the degree of its penetration is measured by the range of the poet's thought or intelligence. And so, indeed, is the coherence of his personality, for " thought is guaranteed by its own laws." It is always an essay in order, in clarification; and that is why it cannot accept the dogmas of character, which would limit its range, or at least confine it to one direction. But the range—the ranging search-light—of the intelligence, its essential mobility, is not to be confused with the vagaries of sentimental-romanticism, or any theory of poetry which pre-supposes the primacy of sentiment—poetry as the direct expression of sentiment. I do not think there is anything in this essay to countenance such a theory. It is contradicted by my insistence on the objective equivalence of the poetic word; it is contradicted also by the implication, everywhere present, of the objec-tive nature of the poet's material—of the worthless-ness of sentiments which are not guaranteed by experience. But more than experience is necessary, for the mind must rise above the realm of existence to the realm of essence, and this can only be achieved by intellectual vision or invention. Santayana, my inspiration in so many loyalties, has expressed this truth with perfect eloquence :

" This incapacity of the imagination to reconstruct the conditions of life and build the frame of things nearer to the heart's desire is dangerous to a steady loyalty to what is noble and fine. We surrender ourselves to a kind of miscellaneous appreciation, without standard or goal; and calling every vexatious apparition by the name of beauty, we become incapable of discriminating its excellence or feeling its value. We need to clarify our ideals, and enliven our vision of perfection. No atheism is so terrible as the absence of an ultimate ideal, nor could any failure of power be more contrary to human nature than the failure of moral imagination, or more incompatible with healthy life. For we have faculties, and habits, and impulses. These are the basis of our demands. And these demands, although variable, constitute an ever-present intrinsic standard of value by which we feel and judge. The ideal is immanent in them; for the ideal means that environment in which our faculties would find their freest employment, and their most congenial world. Perfection would be nothing but life under those conditions. Accordingly our consciousness of the ideal becomes distinct in proportion as we advance in virtue and in proportion to the vigour and definiteness with which our faculties work. When the vital harmony is complete, when the *act* is *pure,* faith in perfection passes into vision. That man is unhappy, indeed, who in all his life has had no glimpse of perfection, who in the ecstasy of love, or in the delight of contemplation, has never been able to say : It is attained.    Such moments of inspiration are the source of the arts, which have no higher function than to renew them."*

Perhaps it is necessary to return in conclusion to a problem raised briefly on an earlier page : the relation of the poet to the objective values of a literary tradition. This problem depends entirely on what we mean by such a phrase.   There is not one literary tradition, but many traditions; there is certainly a romantic tradition as well as a classical tradition, and, if anything, the romantic tradition has the longer history.   As I see the problem it is again a question of intelligence, of that intelligence which is discovered in the perspective of any adequate personality.   It is merely a lack of intelligence to refuse the experience embodied in the poetry of the past; but it shows an even greater lack of intelligence to refuse the experience embodied in the present.   The only duty which the poet has in this matter is to refuse his allegiance to academic *cadres*.   But if we must apply the historical distinctions to this age of ours, we shall find ourselves in a dilemma, for we shall be forced to admit that whilst it is possibly an age of satiety, it is not one of solidity; and if it is certainly an age of stress, we are more doubtful about its energy.    That is to say, it is not clearly either a romantic or a classical age, nor are the categories of a romantic or a classical tradition applicable to it.   In the circumstances the poet has no

* *The Sense of Beauty* (1896), pp. 261-2.

alternative but to rely on "a certain inward perspective," a coherence of the personality based on the widest evidence of the senses.